A Night in Duluth

Other Books by Joe Weil

What Remains (Nightshade Books)

Painting the Christmas Trees (Texas Review Press)

The Plumber's Apprentice (NYQ Books)

West of Home (with Emily Vogel, Blast Press)

The Great Grandmother Light (NYQ Books)

A Night in Duluth

Poems

Joe Weil

The New York Quarterly Foundation, Inc.
New York, New York

NYQ Books™ is an imprint of The New York Quarterly Foundation, Inc.

The New York Quarterly Foundation, Inc.
P. O. Box 2015
Old Chelsea Station
New York, NY 10113

www.nyq.org

First Edition

Set in New Baskerville

Layout by Raymond P. Hammond

Cover Design by Raymond P. Hammond

Cover Photograph by
Marco Muñoz Jaramillo | http://mmjaramillo.wix.com/marcomunozjaramillo

Library of Congress Control Number: 2016933808

ISBN: 978-1-63045-027-4

A Night in Duluth

Acknowledgments

Many of these poems have appeared in or are forthcoming in *The Literati Quarterly, Lips, The Paterson Literary Review, Chicago Quarterly Review, Plume, Big Hammer, This Broken Shore: A Literary Journal, Palisades, Parkways, The Comstock Review, City Lit Rag,* and *Pinelands: An Anthology of Contemporary NJ Poets.*

Contents

A Night in Duluth

For my wife, and two children, Clare and Gabriel,
without whom so many good things would not be possible.

A Poem in Which Lack Is the Necessity of Being

There's someone who's not here,
who probably won't be coming back,
unless the ghost of the number 12 bus
opens its doors with a soft hydraulic hiss.
You remember all the beautiful boredom
of a long summer day—just you and that Spaldeen
you kept whipping against the curb. Above you,
the shadow of the school's flag is performing its
hoochie coochie dance.
Everything in your childhood is lost
to the high weeds of an old man's musings.
What you feel is vital, necessary, beyond
all reproach appears—to the casual witness—
as a pile of junk.
Someone's hand is on your knee.
That was forty years ago.
Someone's calf tightens as they push
down on a pedal, and the Schwinn moves
forward into oblivion.
There are no cows grazing in your
realm of dazed weather, in the bucolic
torpor of the scene—but a woman with a red pistachio
nose leaning out a third story window,
a man entering the dark cool of
a tavern's open door—
Then someone calls your
name, piercing the ribs of four o'clock,
and you throw the Spaldeen with tendon straining oomph
against the street's hard curb,
catching the concrete edge
just so. The ball arcs
high above your head—disappearing
into the cheering silence
where all things perfect go.

The House Where I Was Born

Is missing the roar and rattle of its pipes, the
wheeze of its aging relatives, the groans, and
whines of floor boards, death rattles both
human and otherwise—the tender eyes of
the neighbor's niece watching me fetch the
garbage cans tossed with impressive
brio by burly guys whose lives were thunderous
with routine. The house is sans my mother's Rose
of Sharon, the silver maple out front with its
flock of ugly angry starlings
making various lewd noises—wolf whistles
farts, dog growls—those short tailed, long beaked
birds who shat on every junker Ford we ever parked,
who shat the berries from the Mulberry out back,
those good-for-nothings except breeding
and clogging up the engines of 747's, those
birds I watched for hours as a child from my
parent's bedroom window. That house where I was
born is not my house at all. They've cut
the maples down, replaced the oil burner, stripped the
ugly siding that all the houses on my street once wore
to save on painting costs. They've stripped
the armor of the working class, and left the corpses.
This was my house that stretched
from Lowell to Baltimore—just one enormous Queens.
This was my house, a jump rope at dusk on
a dark street, the children grown to heart attacks and
suburbs. Drive by it, without knowing, until you check
the address. Parking, I raise the tree with my
eyes, restore the Rose of Sharon with my desire.
Everyone who is dead returns and watches me.
Go home, they say, mister, you don't belong.

It Is Hard to Do Anything When You're Poor (Or: Exploding Tulips)

When I was poor, I dreamed the tulips were exploding
on the lawns of our most prosperous citizens:
great mushroom clouds of multi-colored tulips.
Then I felt guilty about wishing death on the rich
and did a nine day novena to St. Jude, and thought
"Well, that's the end of that."
I had kidney stones, bruised ribs, flea bites, lice,
a toothache that sang songs in ancient Greek.
I had hexameters following me around, scribbling
extended metaphors about my various movements
throughout the day. The poor are always suspects. It's
part of our job. The good don't live in sewers.
It was all my own fault. I was lazy. I didn't want
to shovel radioactive tennis shoes—what kind of
ingrate was I? I suppose I was a very bad ingrate.
The worst thing about being poor is you can't go skiing,
or say your plate is full, or have intelligent affairs with
reticent Canadians in stories by Alice Munro.
Late at night, obese, washed up celebrities plead for you
on commercials with wobbly violins, and emaciated
babies. Sooner or later, you look at the shovel,
you look at the radioactive tennis shoes, you look
at the sky, and you say: "Why not? Why the hell not?"
And then you shovel, and keep your mouth shut,
and someone takes a picture of you for a major zine,
and you end up providing fodder for intelligent discussion
on NPR. The good people listen in. They feel that
they understand you, and, yes, the situation. It's all
very clear what must be done, but no one does anything
(that would be extreme).

The tennis shoes never stop mounding to the sky.
The pile never gets smaller. And for that you're grateful.
It's called job security. And, in spite of your one armed children,
everyone is playing soccer on the land mines—and hey,
it's a life.

A Thing I Keep Almost Doing
(For All Those Who Live in the Kingdom of Almost)

I've almost bought a blackberry bush six times in my life,
and on the seventh, carried it all the way up to the register
before plunking it down among some hydrangeas.
I'm sure they need a lot of sun and sand and probably
accident. I have a lot of accidents, but not the kind one
might call *benign neglect*—
for instance, there's that ruined orchard down by the rail yard
where blackberries grow so thick, you could stumble
drunk through a patch, and wake up with a crop in your mouth—
and no one is watching YouTube videos on how to grow them
or doing
much of anything at all except picking the fruit.
I like the way they make a noise in my bucket
and then no noise at all, having just become a fullness,
a glut of bucket berries. I'm getting old and I suppose I should
tackle some weightier subjects, or give this the false weight
of "hidden meanings" but I'm not a pastoral poet. Roll over
Wendell Berry! What I like
about blackberries is they favor the same spots as rusted
bicycle rims, and poison oak, and used condoms, and wayward
shoes, and rain sodden back issues of Ellery Queen:
there, right there where everything is worthless, or, rather, beyond
all worth (there's a difference) in a tangle of sharp and not always
friendly stuff, among the chicory the rancid blankets
of vagrants—this plump ripe fruit, as much a pleasure to the mouth
as those in Eden were, already blessing the corrupted world,
fit only for broken bottle glass, and me.

What Editors Are Looking For Is

No doubt the entrails of birds
on some dust scoured plain—
say a certain masterful
"dryness" mistaken for depth
or perhaps not so much mistaken
as infused with a knowing brittleness—
the kind of brittle you see
on the faces of those who are rarely
if ever pleased—yes—that's it—
a breaking at the corners
of the mouth, at the eyes, a certain
pinched gladness that says:
"I believe this poem and I can
do lunch together. This poem will
not embarrass me should we be
caught in the camera's eye."
I have noticed that the poems
and the editors, and much
of the scenery surrounding
the poems and the editors is
beginning to look the same—
fixed so to speak in an "Excellence"
that does not quite cohere.
I am waiting for a change. Until
then, the birds have dropped
thousands of submissions!
Rivers of wings surround us—
Oh, and vast tribulations.

So Much Aluminum, So Many Flying Houses

After Magritte

I once believed in love at first sight.
I also believed a turtle carried the soul of the world on its back.
Stray voices from some distant planet upheld me.
I was upheld and feverish in my truths.
I wore the peacock's eye, the violent bronze
of the peacock's eye. I was a gong
sounding in all the flowers, a moment's reprieve
between the tail dragged through the dust and the tail unfolding—
a great fan unleashed in the barnyard where they slaughtered the
cattle of the sun. I was the last thing the bull ever saw
before death took away his horns.
I touched what I could—horns, feathers.
The days spoke on my behalf. The hours struck
my chest with their little hammers, then surrendered
to my embrace. Nothing remained of my ambition.
Love grew difficult, if at all. Pianos came to my door
and demanded payment for services rendered.
Overall, it was a good thing I left the world when I did—
so much aluminum, so many flying houses.

Dialing the Light

A flower is in the field.
I am using passive verbs
to tether it to ground.
The dark over its crown
is sprinkled with stars,
planets, occasional meteors,
a plane in which my dead travel,
throbs ceaselessly over
the houses where snores
and groans, both of pain
and of pleasure, emit a sort of
ongoing gas.
This is what I breathe—
the gassy hum, the low cry
from the streets. It has no home, no
origin, I can point to it and say
"There!" That's where my
grief began. Forget it.
Start over: I am passed
pleasing any poetry aesthetic.
Here they all fail: all my P's gather
to pop at the mic, to explode
into a sound my throat
refuses to claim.
It is your own throat, too—
moaning, though you
swear it is not your own.
The flower shakes every wind.
Its roots are a vast city.
In the plane, the dead have
no window seats. The movie
shows my face—four hundred
replicas of me and each
one unable to—it is enough
to say unable to. What has

been snarled, snagged like
this—and so often, is
known only by its snags.
This face, and the puckered
thumb I hold to my children's
foreheads—to mark them with ash.
I, too, have a plane to catch.

This flower, if you could
ever approach it, exists
in a field where snow is falling
but not sticking—a wet field,
a ground swell, a stone confounding
meadow. This place where stones
tumble and hiss and thaw, and
the flower emits a signal
in the reek of that mud—it is
singing, far from the vast
city of its roots, sun—wanton
its axis of petals
turned just so to
dial the light—at 5,
at 12, at 2. It is alive. It would
have me come, my boots half
sinking in the mud and
praise it.

What Does It Mean to "Snow in my Heart?"

One of my students writes "she snows in my heart"
and I kind of like that—in spite of myself—
or is it *despite* myself?
Quick! I'm losing rules. It is
snowing in someone's heart. The flakes
fall like the long eye lashes of the dead.
If we could glimpse the dead as they look
on that other plane, they'd all have long
white eyelashes, and every time they blinked
down it would fall—that kind of snow which
is beautiful but doesn't stick at all, say, on
a late March morning when the forsythia
has begun to bloom and its crayon
yellow wands drape the edges of drive ways.
O Daughters of Jerusalem, I charge thee
by the love I bear to tell the landscapers
not to shear them off! A little drooping death
never hurt a poor boy.

It's what makes the pretty strange, and the strange
most strangely beautiful, and now I understand
how someone or something can snow in
a heart. The student's life is full of misspellings
and faulty sentences—and so is mine:
my life is a construction site where the money
ran out and everything has been left: half a wall,
a couple of orange cones, some caution tape,
the yellow of forsythia, a thick sheet of
plastic flapping in the wind. A friend took a
photo of a thick sheet of plastic flapping in
the wind. It made the whole world behind it
ghostly—like figures walking in a landscape
by Turner. It made the world translucent—
the way it really is, for there is a veil between us
and the covenant.

Let it be torn. We don't really see. If we did
why would we need to write poems? I am writing
this poem and when I am done, there will be a
forsythia bush, the one from my childhood, so big
and grown so wild, I could eat lunch in the fairy
circle of its arms. I'll watch the snow from there.
The eyelash snow that dies as soon as it is born—
the lashes falling through space, falling on my
tongue, my eyelids—the first true baptism,
and then? All that comes to die in my heart
will rise, and send forth a thousand shoots,
the branching arms of Shiva—all of them blooming.

Poor

It is hard to make a living
when so many others are also
trying to make a living.
It's like reaching for the same torch
and you say: well, I'd grab the end of the flame,
but it burns. Yikes! Let me grab
the handle, but sixteen million hands
all with pinky rings are grabbing the handle
and you need to break all those fingers,
smash them, cut them off just to
get a decent grip—and then you find out
that's not even the right torch, is it?
See what I mean? It's hard to
make a living. Much easier to make
a dying, but everyone does that
well, and perfectly, and without
even trying (most of the time).
I want to make paper airplanes but
I forgot how. Last night I stayed up
weeping with a whole shit load of
paper in my hands. See? You're
good, you're good, but you're never
good enough and you never will be
and that's when you need
a Dutch uncle, a friend in high places,
one of those suckers who owns
all the matches with which the
torches burn. Can you see them
burning? It is late and thousands
of torch bearers are proceeding
up and down the space just outside
your grasp. And you hear yourself crying:
please. Is that your voice? And you
feel how wet the pavement is when
you kneel on it, and how everything

cracks inside you, and the
smart ones post tweets about how
complicated it all is. It isn't fucking
complicated! It's called mercy—
you don't need ten thousand
terminal degrees to achieve it.
You don't need to go on and on
with your "complications." It's called
mercy. I heard it would rather
die than turn men into asses,
but that might be just the
real mercy. Right now I'd settle
for the fake. Give me the
business end of the torch, fellas—
come on. Hand it over.
I don't mind burning
for a good cause. I've been
burning my whole life. *Give it here.*

Morning Lauds

Woke up too damned early—
nothing to do except
make sure others
stay unconscious.
My house bursts into furnace sounds,
the heat working overtime,
moving through these walls.
Outside: old snow, new snow,
the bear I imagine lives
in the wood shed.
Every time I retrieve a log,
it's my version of "into
the breach." Heart pounding.
The stars over this house
are not bad—there's Orion!
There'd be a lot more
if the city didn't leave its lights on.

All night below me,
people screwing wildly and often.
God bless them!
Just thinking about it,
the yawp of the bed springs
puts a smile on my face.
Go for it, peoples!
Be oblivious to the stars.
We have so many other forms of entertainment
these days—like texting.
I am growing old, I think.
My arm hurts, my back hurts.
My body is beginning
to make its turn toward death.
But *death* sounds too abstract.
No one *dies*. That's a word
we have for falling down and not getting up.

All that fucking and starlight
and millions of more stars in the
glimmer of the fresh snow on
the juniper and the holly berry.
I have juniper. I have holly berry.
You'd think I was a nature poet.
This isn't a nature poem. If so,
its stanzas would be neat.
I woke
up at 3:30, with not even my bladder to blame.
I can't put on the television.
Little children will awaken.
I can't even turn on a light.
My son, a year and some change,
should stir soon. Cradling him in the dark
I will say: when you get older,
bless the people who are fucking in the village.
That is my spiritual advice.
Bless them all. And the ones who are
fuckless? Dream they are dormant gods
and only lolling, like an inward sea.
Bless them, too. Give your enemies
a blessing. Say: "Blessing! Blessing!"
No one will be up to call you
corny or maudlin.
Forget them, or rather, bless them,
too. Go out to the woodshed
to feel the bear in the dark,
pawing your life, leaving
the dark stain of its claw on your
frontal lobes. This is no celebrated bear.
It's all yours. You own it. Remember I
loved you more than blessing. It is
easy to do what Whitman did. It is
so much harder to fail the way I am failing,

with my tongue spouting nonsense,
with you in my arms.
Little truck monster!
Duke of Earl. I wish I could show you
a thousand telephone booths
with their preternatural light.
They existed once when I was your age.
They were even out on the plains.

You had to walk toward them
the way you walk toward deities.
At this hour, you didn't wait for your turn.
No one was there except the bodies
of sleeping cars.
You became the night, and the sleeping hills
and the soft moans of people fucking.
And you didn't care about harsh diction.
The dime sounded great going down in the slot.
The dial made a beautiful click.
For me, it was mercy. What will be
mercy for you? I love you more than
a telephone booth at 3 am,
more than the voices of all my dead. It
is so hard for me to love you this much.
It means I have to stay alive.

For Cassandra

Not having been heard
as if a waterfall, invisible, yet ever roaring
had fallen between her and the world;
and having been seen only in her coat of motley,
she moved as a crooked thing moves
scrabbling, scuttling, the whole of her day
spent tripping over the knottiest roots;
and when she died, when the waterfall ceased—
they heard her silence. This they filled
with their own voice—the common
tongue that licks the salt from prophets
until nothing is left but a stain.
She lived as one you might think harmlessly insane.
Catastrophe, she cried, *Catastrophe*—
while the sea kept up its lifting and falling mood.
Catastrophe—cries the soul—in solitude.

Losing a Cell Phone in Sioux City

Maybe it fell into the void of someone's eye.
I tipped the cleaning lady a fin
(she didn't take it).
Perhaps it is hanging with
Gogol's runny nose, or has decided to
camp out in his mangy over coat:
there amid the after dinner mints,
the ticket stubs to a government
inspector. Who knows?
I had a hundred pictures of my children
ready to download. The falls on
the Sioux river, a panther with a kitten
clutched in its mouth, made of
copper, poised outside the Hotel Hilton.
Panther, find my phone! Bring it hence like your kitten
back to room 809. Return my children to me.
Bring back the sound of falls.
I'm a fat fool in suspenders. I have diabetes,
hypertension, delusions of grandeur. I'm
more than 500 miles away from home
(Fie Peter, Paul, and Mary).
Do you hear me? Forever holding in thy maw
what's dear to thee
there—in jaws that bring down deer,
the answering service prattles on in Spanish
and English. Dawn is coming, a steak grease
stain in the east. Soon everything will be
medium rare. The sky will erupt. The Panther will
pose where the smokers
dawdle, their cigarettes clenched. Everything
waits to leap, to saunter forth—to lose what
this panther knows is unbearable:
Clare spinning on a table, Gabriel, crawling into
words, all the words he will ever need, the splash
of consciousness. Where the hell is my brain—its
cells dying, all its children—*lost?*

The Wasp Inside the Spider

Dreams took me down.
I was killed by dreams.
So I quit dreaming.
I noticed the bugs
in the grass, and learned
their names, their genus,
learned the trees, the small
intimacies of plant matter,
the way the oak holds
toxins in its fallen leaves
that kill the seeds of other
plants—how perhaps, late at
night, the oak is plotting—
scheming and scamming, and
the spider is weaving its web.
But there is a wasp, microscopic,
which crawls into the DNA of spiders
and gets them to weave
square webs instead of round.
And when this has been done, the
larvae hatch and feed on spiders.
The web must have a certain
tensile strength—which the
square provides. I am tired
of strength.
I have been strong and have
eaten my way through
things. I am made
palpable by stones, by the dark
world beneath rocks,
in the mold, in the damp.
I swear it's all true. You
can look it up. Get out your
smartphones. It is like
a dream. Parts of it are
always missing.

Parable at the Greasy Spoon

For Stan Laurel

The days are all burgers
and then one afternoon
there's a fly in your soup
and you don't remember
ordering soup, but
there it is! French onion,
and just the way you would
like it (if you liked French
Onion soup). You don't
want to be a pest, certainly,
but you say: "Waiter, there's a
fly in my soup," and the waiter
says: "You ordered a burger."
And you say: "I *know...*"
Then both of you scratch
your heads for a long while
and begin to blubber.
The world is indeed full of
soup, and wasn't it Kafka
who wrote: "the soup went
in search of a fly"?
You don't know why
but you lift the fly on
your soup spoon and
think: Perhaps I was
meant to eat this fly.
You swallow it. It has
a thousand eyes, or close
to that number and can
turn its head in endless circles
like a tiny airport.
The waiter returns with your
new soup—French onion—
just as you like it, sans fly.

And that's how habits change:
you eat what perhaps must
be swallowed. You are given
what you never ordered. You
douse it with pepper, some
hot sauce, oyster crackers.
The cheese in the soup is
nicely browned on the top,
the onions savory in the broth.
What the hell? The fly strobes
the darkness inside you. He
speaks several languages. He
is a poet, and each of his eyes
are scanning the rib cage
where the heart chews what it has
been given to chew; where it
beats wildly in space, where it
pounds out a beat, strong and
wondrous, in the kingdom of flies.

Things I Hate

Hate being busy
hate others going on and on about being busy
hate the business of being busy
hate how people in America are even busy
being reflective.
Hate the schedules of reflection.
Hate the fucking schedules
hate the lists, the doing of this
and the undoing of that
hate that I can't lick a freckle from my nose
and swallow it and turn into a field of wild mushrooms
hate that no one ever gives me a big waxy turnip
and says: "Here pal, here's a big
waxy turnip."
Hate that all the good surprises
in my life lie behind me like so many
run over squirrels—their fluffy tails
combed by the wind, crushed by
an 18 wheeler driven by an asthmatic who
has a pair of lucky sunglasses
(which he just lost)
hate that some positive thinker might
stand in the middle of this poem and say:
"How do you know all the good surprises
in your life lie behind you?"
Hate that I can't crush injustice
like a can of Fresca, hate Fresca,
hate that I don't really hate injustice,
hate most abstractions—the word excellence
for example, or goal-oriented, or
appropriate, or any of those words
that have lost their eyes, and hands, and
can't feed you, or kiss you or offer you
a big waxy turnip when you need one,
hate that I hate this poem but can't stop

until the hate exhausts itself in
a barrage of very real emotional
anguish, with me lying
on the floor staring up at the blue conveyor
belt of the sky, wondering when
the good god fuck
that belt will break and the machinery
of the cosmos
will come to a grinding halt, with me,
somehow still alive, calmly punching out, and
getting a beer, or, if not a beer,
then a rib eye steak sandwich
from the White Diamond in Roselle Park,
New Jersey, where, if you tell the fry cook
the sky has broken,
he'll say: "Damn...well it sure lasted a long time;
you want raw onions or fried with that?"

Status Report

The Eurobros are slipping into unconsciousness.
There is a boat leaving the port of your dreams
full of fish heads and back copies of Ellery Queen.
Fortuitous signs are appearing all over the world.
Last night, I glimpsed the sign of Exxon. Then I
saw Shell up ahead. All that yellow in the dark
made me sad. I parked near a star glutted field
full of Timothy grass and the severed heads
of dolls and I sang the Oscar Meyer wiener
song in a low voice—directly at the belt
of Orion. It did me no good. The recent geniuses
are right. Epiphanies don't really happen.
You're out in a field trying to address the gods
and you start thinking about mice or
oral sex and whether you ever gave head
to get rid of someone. You would like
to get rid of yourself without suicide—
a sort of starry placating. You'd like to
fall off the cliff just before the entourage
catches you and tumble 100 feet into
dark waters where the nymphs await—
glow worms, fusion of floating fish sperm
and egg—glimmer, glimmer,
vast colonies of flotsam and jetsam.
What do you think longing is?
Have you ever wrestled the intangible angel?
When an abstraction breaks your hip,
what can you do but limp? I have
loved my way into countless bone
fractures. I don't need to apologize.

I Am Sick of the Whole Apparatus; Give Me a Pretzel

It is Sunday. There is fog
in the leper colony at Amherst.
Big animals roam the plains.
This is called parataxis.
If I do this long enough
will an egret appear?
I hate egrets. (They're so tacky).
I heard you can win prizes
by learning to care about...
I forgot what it is I am supposed
to care about. Do *you* know?
Oh, little things.
Is that it?
I care about you.
I've been practicing all week.
The snow is on the mattress
and the mattress is outside in the snow.
Perhaps the window is open.
Then the mattress is inside.
There is snow on the mattress
inside. I am trying not to
use the word "and." It might
make things more complicated if I did.
Forget talent. Embrace genius.
Only the right people know what genius is.
Everyone knows what talent is.
Do you want to be everyone?
Of course not! Lighten up, sweetie.
With the right people
you can be a genius.
Skip the talented part.
I made you! You make me.
You go first: call me a genius
in a big magazine. I'll do the same.

Let's ignore the waiter.
He wants us to leave a tip.
He believes in talent.
He believes in *a job well done.*
Ignore him. He'll go away.
If not, stone him.
It's very spiritual.
Have you ever stoned anyone?
At first, you sometimes miss.
Then the party gets going.
Your first solid hit is really incredible.
After that, it's fairly routine.

On the Birthday of Sir Isaac Newton

Things fall and there's a reason. (Thanks, Mr. Newton!),
but I had a dream last night gravity had failed me. My
children were floating away toward the sun. My wife's coffee
was fleeing her mug and her dark hair trailed behind her
like a comet's tail. I was holding on to a heavy hide-a-bed
shouting: Stop! As if an imperative sentence could do the
trick. Stop! I always hated hide-a-beds, especially when I
moved furniture for a living. Damned things were heavy
with steel, usually on the top floor, and they often opened
while you lifted them, even though you'd tied string around
their mechanisms. They gashed your fingers, left scuff
marks, gouge marks, blood; that's if they didn't knock you
down the stairs. The doors were always too narrow. If you
managed to get the monster shoved out into sunlight and
into the new house, it refused to open. Hide-a-beds resent
being both fully couch and fully bed. They are the furniture
version of the Anti-Christ. But I digress. Now here I was
clinging to my nemesis for "dear life," like Sidney Poitier
and Tony Curtis in that movie about two men forced to flee
together—each chained to the other, escaped fugitives. I
thought: Hide-a-bed, don't fail me now! That's when my
children floated by. Gabriel said: "Hi, Da" in his one year
old's voice. Clare, said "Oh, oh." I tried to abandon the
hide-a bed to follow them but I was tied to it by a long,
winding chord, and then gravity came back, as they say,
with a vengeance, looking for justice. I was falling tethered
to that evil double life. I woke up with a thud far removed
from Hide-a beds, checked on my sleeping children, felt my
sleeping wife's leg under the covers. I came to the comput-
er to find out it was Sir Isaac Newton's birthday! So, happy
birthday, Sir Izzy! Thank God it was an apple and not a
hide-a -bed that found your genius skull.

I Want to Lick Your Knee and Weep for Rahoon

The knee is like the ball of a walnut banister,
the kind you hold onto as you glide down
into the final chapter of an Edith Wharton novel
where the class system and its ugly graciousness
has gutted you, but, still you glide,
smiling, poised, kissing the cheeks of those
who have condemned you to social death.
I like that kind of knee, Emily!
I never expected to marry someone who rhymed with knee.
Maybe Meg with leg, or Flo with toe, but ah!
In my head now, I can see the prose of Wharton,
Henry James' best pupil, and I can see your name
and yet the winter dusk (which is months away)
reminds me of Rahoon, which somewhere in Joyce is wept over.

Where the fuck is Rahoon? Or who? For all my pedantry I never
"looked it up." In North Carolina, a woman has been
pressured to resign for not having the proper kudos
for a laureate. All over the world, gate keepers are assigning
elitist honors to populist posts.
And I am sad. I read her poem and it is pretty bad
but not as bad as the one who attacked her. All the poems
are bad—this one, too, and the bread is sad.
Lord have mercy on us! But let me get back to your knee:
When I was little, the world on Saturday
smelled of lemon pledge, and shone so that my face
smiled from door knobs, counters, banisters,
and I rubbed myself like a happy cat, tail up
against all surfaces, all bright things
and saw my distorted fun house mirror face in the faucet's chrome,
and laughed, and saw the sky in gallant tatters,
and then I grew and learned to ignore the magic
for an established order—which would never
stoop as I am stooping now to kiss your knee and cry.
Here, children are being blown to smithereens.

Here, poets are turned to swine.
Your knee is hard and smooth and tanned
and I am sick of everything but adoration. Lick!
Come down the
stairs—oh indomitable spirit! Weep for Rahoon
and let me kiss your hand.

A green brick

in the hot kiln of summer—green brick
of the vegetation, green man hidden
in the sentences of sleep, beyond all harm
you came to me and sounded no alarm
except the jay's fierce and unbidden
cry—that voice, like the kick
of deer's hooves against window glass—
sudden, a breaking of storm
in the full court press of the rain
against all roofs, forbidden, and in vain
we struggled, caught in the thick
webbed memory—the warm
embrace of whatever it was we built:
that full tilt of stars above the drunken boat house,
the heron's mating in cattails along the shore.

/

Do You Understand Why I Am Dying?

I miss my friend Dave Roskos.
Sometimes I daydream we are walking
stooped under the shadow of summer trees
and he sees a gas station up ahead and says:
"Joe, let's get some coffee." Nothing monumental.
We share some of our dead. They rise in us.
Usually we ignore them. The best way is to order some
shrimp fried rice, watch a cult movie like "Joe."
Listen to Albert Ayler's Marches. The Poetry
establishment suddenly name drops Ayler—as if
he were trying to be innovative, but he was just
playing the brass bands he heard in his head,
and if that's innovative, so be it.
I would like to think, if Albert Ayler was
walking with us, he'd have said: "let's get some coffee"
or stood with us near the tidal flats
pissing into the reeds. The other day, I took a piss
that lasted a full minute and a half. I was amazed and
wanted to share it with my friends, but most of them were
dead, and Dave was an ocean away, and my wife Emily
whom I love, said: *wow* while she changed
our daughter's diaper.
I want Emily with us, in a bright kitchen, laughing.
Sometimes I want to walk with her on the last decent day
of the year, both of us in sweaters, and not say anything—
just listen to the gulls, watch them scavenge, and then I want
to smell her hair on my fingers and tell her: do you understand
why I am dying? Why do all these numb nut mother fuckers
think I'm negative? But it is a sweetness, a sweetness itself,
the voice of God that drives me crazy—and the brass band I hear
is coming down the beach, combing the waves with its dissonant
celebrant waking—the seagulls, the longing: I tell you and I tell me,
to miss anyone is a blessing, a mitzvah, the highest.
I am grateful for all I miss, including my wife who, even in my arms
is a longing for friends whose words I can no longer hear.

How Do I Write to Duluth?

Duluth, you were always yellow on my maps
and a town in vaudeville
and no one had died yet, or fallen down
in the dusk of their irredeemable sadness.
Duluth, I am irredeemably sad.
Duluth, I kept forgetting which state
you were in and so you kept floating above
baseball diamonds and parking lots and
the gay farmer who went to dangerous bars late at night
to be held in some other hayseed's arms.
And why is everyone queer, or straight in some
awful way? And why do I wish I had dragged my body
like a song, or a pen across the continent,
scrawling your name?
Duluth, I don't want to be Richard Hugo.
I don't want to be Hart Crane.
Fred Astaire danced with his sister across your best stage—
the A circuit of vaudeville. Duluth, if God lifted me
in the grain elevator of his wrath and poured me forth,
all the grain would have whispered praise.
Duluth, you know. I am no Allen Ginsberg.
Anaphora comes cheap. I have no money.
I am paying for you with my repetitions:
Duluth, which I often misspelled Deluth, you are
no doubt nothing much to see. Neither am I.
You have to open me up and live under the dark trees
of my homeliness, and then, oh my God! But I am
a green pocketbook, a blessed event of nothing—
the cricket chirping of a man who has walked beyond hope
and the furthest city light—
but that's someone else's poem. Everything I love is borrowed,
stolen, including you—this watch fob I carry and shine with
the worn elbow of my shirt. Duluth, you wear the patina
of my grief and wonder. You are the last cricket in November
singing without a reason—loudly in the closet
where a dead man's shoes have all been polished.

Serenity Prayer

Dawn at Gary's confectionery,
big fake thunder of the metal grate being raised.
Paper truck belly flops its load
of star ledgers at the entrance
and then, recedes into diesel fumes.
We collate sections, first customer, an old guy
wearing a cream colored fedora,
a tropical shirt, brown penny loafers.
He scans the headlines,
presses change gently into my palm.
I admire the veins in his scrawny arms,
his face so tan, all hide and cheek bones.
He doesn't enter the store.
The first six customers never do,
but chat us up as we fold in the gentle light—
Venus, morning star, and the
half-moon above frame houses dissolving.
We work at the stacks,
carry them inside. I sit with a
half-assed cup of coffee.
No need for a good one.
This is 1972, in a galaxy far away from
baristas. I am 14, happy as Jesus among his elders.
Kidding and being kidded,
the scent of Aqua Velva and Old Spice,
Dutch Masters and Bay Rum aftershave—
among old men who have decided the world
is going to hell—but not just yet.

The Hammer of Nineveh

What is the sound of a hammer to
an America that emits only the chipper peeps of tulips?
And all of them half full (Oh, never empty tea cups),
filled with the rain of providence?
The tulips are emitting sounds
from mer to merde; it is the smallest range—
this tweakiling through the short cropped grass, this
positive land—this kitschy corsage of "words to live by"
which prattle every wind: keep it lite, shop right,
be blessed by whatever wisdom songs
are playing in the tropes. These hopes, these
cute epiphanies that shop, that have
no cousin in the moon. That have no kith, no kind.
That range from mer to merde—this cheerful idiot
and blind.

Depression

You might begin with eagles.
People will tell you eagles can cure you,
especially if they're soaring high
in the azure (it's always in the azure, isn't it?)
to some sort of elevator muzak
version of Philip Glass—
a kind of "Smooth Glass,"
a glass that can't ever cut you
or sever your arteries.
Removed from all danger, you'll
push serenity into your schedule:
an hour or so a day of mindfulness.
But suppose the underlying
cause is your culture sits on four billion
tons of violence, on a black body
become a discourse
that makes you wince into apologetics.
Have you ever asked: Do I have a right
to be happy? And what is that lizard
high on the rock—that sun licking mother fucker
who pharma and military, and spiritual
"transport" have all failed to realize?
Forget him.
Kneel to your purpose.
It is not what you think it is.
It was never that thing that you were busy doing.
It's small, and has tentacles—a sort of
livid purple, quivering in mid-air
like the dandelion's roots you spent all morning
digging up so that the neighbors might say:
"nice people live there." I swear there is
a scream coming from your chimney.
Your children heard it. They leaned into the wind
and were turned to salt.

I Was Born Stupid

I was born stupid,
listing to one side
with my tongue
hanging out—lolling
as they say—a lollygag.
I appeared "listless"
even though I was
listing, and noticeably
so. "Look at that listing baby,"
the fates said, "he's about
to capsize!" They cut the thread.
Yes, I was snipped. It was on
a waning moon. And soon
folk realized I would not
be playing Mozart's Rondo
in C any time soon, nor would
I give a credible performance
in math, or spelling, or home economics
and since drooling was not considered
a skill, I received no credit
for being a drooling idiot.
I grew to epic stupidity.
The carp spoke to me
from the deep river mud.
I was sent into the forest to die
and came back carrying a set
of dishes which I dropped
and which smashed
upon entering the village.
Each shard became a balloon
floating above the church steeple
and out of the balloons came the
secrets of the town's people.
To make a long story *longer,*
they blamed me, and so I was killed

and planted in an unmarked
grave from which the Lilac grew.
Yes, I am an origin of Lilacs.
In the spring, at this hour,
my fragrance is everywhere,
like a rumor.
Do you think the clever ever have anything
to do with flowering?
I suppose they do. They slaughtered me,
and I grew.

Death Song 1

for Walt

I remember being a poet.
It was in another life beside
railroad tracks and bodies of
distended water, among
broken moorings, bulkheads
rusted bolts from the Iron Age.
Bridges that burned silver
in the morning hoarfrost. I was
a poet and sang like a winch
to a dirty mass of ropes—
all stretched to wave's lap
and tidal swoon. I reeked
of swamp gas, and creosote,
fish slime and the salted
slate of roofs. I was
if not happy there, then sad in
an exultant way—lung sad,
breathing out the notes of
sirens, lured to my death
but tied to the mast of life.
And when the fog horn and
the train whistle sounded
I knew how to shut up
and bow my head to the
greater singer—songs of
whatever sounds in the infinite
cry of birds, the harsh
beautiful low down cadences
of whatever it is that
called me into words
and back again.

Death Song 2

for William

What would be more like hell
than to go on caring about you—
your cities and your laundry detergents,
your applause and your jeers, the
silence of your ungodly indifference?
I care about the bend in that river—
the scraggly mess of staghorn sumac
snow bearded along its shore—the way it turns
and twists in memory passed factories
and graveyards.
And not even that.
It is no longer a matter of caring.
Last night, my chest keened
and I had no strength to lift my children.
Let the wind lift them. Let all the advisers
leave the scene of this accident.
I see my kids being blown
in the maelstrom, striving and being
driven. Whatever is driven, tossed,
untethered, flung—
good. It is as it should be. Justice
is just another word for sleep.
Sleeping, a man is worth the whole world.

Death Song 3

for Emily

To be discounted—like road kill
and yet the wind so powerfully
in your fur, and the sunlight, too,
to be something the child wished
the father would have stopped to stare at:
What animal? Not a deer or a
possum, but something stranger—
so strange that the car should have
had to stop, should have
ceased its traveling, and the father
and son piled out to know,
to know against all lanes
the animal that it was... *this self*
grown outward—like a prayer.

Farewell (Again)

I've given up poetry
and I've written a poem
to tell you that.
See? It's in tercets!
Oh I forgot. Tercets were
popular ten years ago.
I've given up poetry
because I am so ten years ago,
and ten years ago, I was so—well—
you get my drift. I'm Nixon
and I'm letting you know you
won't have me to kick around
anymore. I've already failed.
Success and death are the two
things I've never experienced
and something tells me death
is more likely. If I die, ten poets
will remember me for an evening
while a cappuccino maker whirs
too loudly and that
will be my success.
In America,
poverty is shot, processed
and performed as a cautionary tale.
I wanted to be a good writer.
I didn't have the money needed
to go to grad school and
get told how to write,
how to snub, how to schmooze.
I have very little talent, but I can
feel it in my bones when I
hold my children. How can so
much love go into a man
so mediocre that he'd actually
tell the truth about his hurts

and refuse to keep silent?
I am intelligent enough
to know this will "damage my
career" such as it is, but, if
you are dying in tercets,
you may as well damage something.
I never wanted a career.
I wanted to say:
Look, the sky's been handcuffed
to a rose! I was a lousy tool grinder.
Even worse than a poet.
Frauds should have no children.
My greatest sin was wanting.
It is hard not to want. You have
to be a very great poet not to
want. I know that.
You have to have the strength to
bite off your own leg, to escape
the steel jaws of your ego.
I am trying to do that.
I am trying to embarrass myself
so as to die in the only good way—
to be clean somehow, to wash this shit
from my mouth. To stop
feeling evil. I hate the poetry scene.
It is not why I came into the world.
It is not why God showed me
how bees circle the holes of sugar dispensers
or how the detritus on beaches, the word
detritus, the very word itself,
is lovely and sane and supports
the twin pillars of heaven. I am sick.
It is hard to want and be sick.
Yeats already mentioned that.
I came into the world to be—

to be slaughtered, but I forgot
to be childless, to be expendable.
I write this poem so that my children
will understand. I loved them. It
is nothing incredible. It is
a bowl of sugar encircled by bees
in a diner where the food
may not have been very good, and the service
stank. I spent my life in such places.
I put my eye to the hole
and looked for a world full of hives,
the soft sound near the sweetness
I knew. I could be stung
and maybe it was worth it. Who knows?
I want my children to believe
it was worth the whole bloody world to
understand how even a word could rise
Detritus, which is what I will leave,
Detritus, road paved with good
intentions (and little life insurance),
shells, drift wood, condoms,
needles, dead crabs, weed sop,
the cry of hungry birds. What else
can you leave them?
Sans good poems, a lot of
bad ones. My palm on the back
of their skulls, gentle
the way I never was.

Night Swinging

Homeless, I sat on a swing at 2 AM, feeling my body
sag into that yielding bow—that strap of leather. Hands gripped,
held rusted chains, feet pushed the needle in—
to punch a hole through space, to sew it, seal it
tight around my body. What despair I felt I knew was mine—
not some philosopher's, not some bleak code of cool
that I had learned to use—not shit faced drunk, not high,
not "not"—just this: the night air frisked me, and
finding no weapons, led my poverty to whatever cat's
cradle realm had become my "home."
A body wholly body dressed in rags, I found
the point where jumping off was jumping in
to whatever pile of dead leaves might break the fall.
What broke my fall? Am I still falling? Power is
a gift for letting go, at just that moment
when the weapon grows enormous in your hand:
and you disdain it, not because you're kind,
but just because an arbitrary god might cross
the threshold of your consciousness and sing
a nursery rhyme, or Marvin Gaye, and in the midst
of suffering you laugh, and in the midst of laughter
the whole earth slams you shut—and there you've landed,
a churl of gravity, deaf, dumb, and blind,
sprawled out inconstant beneath the inconstant moon.

Everybody Used Me (A Poem of Codependent Bliss)

The poets used me.
The wee people under the sighs of enormous mushrooms used me.
Lovers used me.
What was I to do? I said to the North Sea: just be cold and forget
about any favors. The North Sea kissed my feet and I used it.
All this using...what does it amount to? The dead heroin
addict behind door number two is beyond all using.
The dead goldfish providing its own scum to the surface of waters
is useless and beyond all using. Me? On a bed of nails staring up
at the constellation Scorpio, a sweet gum leaf pressed
against my mouth—like a dust mask, like a disguise—like, well,
like a sweet gum leaf is beyond all using.
Fall, sweet gum leaf, with your five fingered dawn!
Fall, so that rubbing your stem, I will be crushed into scent.
All the users...I am only sad I'm no longer of any use.
Here: here's a Pilsner. Do you know what you're doing?
I know the more subtle dolphins balance glittering dimes
instead of balls on their noses. Wallace Stevens' wife supplied
the profile. Everyone is unhappy but longing like the snow
that falls on the bog of Allen, that digs up the corpse of Cathy,
and, if not, what the hell? Everyone used me and when it was
over I said: but come back! I have a spatula. I can make omelets!
I never said they were good omelets. But somehow, everyone knew.

Beyond the Longed for Thing

There were piebald horses and piebald snow,
the deep ruts of the mud as the winter thawed,
and I thought: there are three trees, and a rock,
and the scrapings of antlers against the Beech.
What can God teach except beyond the
longed for thing? If you should hear the scratching
of the fox sparrow in the leaves, know I am there,
where the fox sparrow grieves. Beloved, the stink
of the fallen leaves means nothing except
that I am halt and lame before the covenant wind.
Brush the hair of my martyred bones,
the highway of lost ones. Let me know
that I wear a crown of thorns.

From a Book of the Poor

When I was a child, I mean truly a child in age as well as all
that other stuff, my family was poor, and though we had at
least six televisions, they were all black and white portables,
and half of them had sound and the other half had a pic-
ture, and a third of them had six channels (but you needed
a match book stuck in the channel changer to hold them in
place). Every once in a while, you'd get channel six which
in North East Jersey was Philly and the south. I loved that
because I'd get something different for a change, but for
the most part, channel six was just a blizzard of fuzz. One
day I held a Bic pen—the translucent kind—to my eye, and
due, to the miracle of prisms, Anne Margaret's hair turned
truly red, and Peter Ustinof was playing his cowardly noble
functionary role in gold, and, to my own warped sense of
life, I had found a way to have colored television! All my
friends mocked me because I made the mistake of telling
them, but a girl who was part of the Cuban exile and didn't
stay long (her father died and she moved to Florida) came
over my house one afternoon to watch *Dark Shadows* with
me, and when she saw that I was holding the pen to my eye,
she laughed, and said: "I do that, too!" And she kissed me
full on my mouth (we were both 9 and so the kiss was mostly
the bone of jaw against bone). To be understood in your
poverty, fully known is the whole meaning of the law—final-
ly and beautifully understood and not judged. Either that's
true, or so what? We can move on to the next epiphany, the
next gadget. Her leg rubbing against mine—the motion of
sad, autumnal crickets.

Despair

It's too big a concept to take seriously.
I mean, the whole 20th century played in it:
a big fat sand box full of green bottle glass.
The bottle glass was nice—even when it cut you.
You could put that glass to your eye and
watch the world become a sort of
leeched emerald—the coke bottle green
that sometimes fills the sky before a major storm.
But nothing major ever happens anymore—or even minor.
It's all one blue note—between modes of being
and not being. Forget all that "to be or not to be."
Though the culture is a choice culture, all
the gears have seized somewhere in the middle
and even the elephants on the plains are disaffected.
And the rhinos have learned to be snide.
And they all live somewhere with six roommates
who label their foods, when they aren't out
eating something new. Everyone wants something
new. I don't. What are going to do with it
except make it old?
All my old loves gather 'round me,
and I don't mean lovers—I mean the umbers,
the magentas, the color of rain water, the sound
of gas from a burner—all of it ascending
like precocious children in a Spielberg flick,
bikes back lit by suburban skies glutted with stars.
They gather round and keep the vultures at bay.
They are saying: rise. Despair is for glum detectives
in Graham Greene novels. Yes, it's true. I have
pencils—freshly sharpened. I can eat corn chowder
all I want except it will kill me. In the rain
they are chanting a mass by Palestrina.
It has not been sponsored by a church. I've
heard rumors certain souls are so sick
they've started singing, and Palestrina just pours

out of them—an inward groaning of the spirit.
Have you heard the choirs chanting as they pass?
Sometimes, they assume the forms of strangers.
Sometimes they are dead children, and we take out
the word tragic, and wipe off the moth balls
and enter the memes of our lies. I want to say
"I'm a liar!" and have the chanting stop—
the way a life stops when you shoot it:
no chanting, no circles of aesthetics to make
the medicine go down, no silence full of candles.
On the walls of the city Andromache shouts
"Hector! Here is my desolation!" But that's a poem.
Here, the roommate has left a note to her mates:
Someone ate my mango mousse. No offense, but that sucks.
And it does. All around her, on a thousand screens
they are showing looters, and burning Toyotas and
commercials for Revlon, and previews of the next
season of this and that, and it's raining. She thinks:
if people weren't so...so selfish, and someone should teach
the black children how to smile, and how to wear
like, penny loafers, or something, and then one of those
ignorant white cops, one of those Walmart types, wouldn't be so
trigger happy. It's all about appearances, isn't it?
Of course, those kids make her nervous, too, when
she walks past a liquor store on her way to the bakery,
and they're looking at her ass. She's so sure they're
looking at her ass. Those kids love big asses. And
for a white girl, she's got a big one. It's not
like, out of shape, but it's *big*. You could put your
pint of micro-brew on it, and come back later
and it would still be there. Yes. She's got a big
ass, and everyone wants her. Doesn't everyone
want skinny white girls with big asses? People
ought to be honest. Everyone is scared of
those kids—they're so menacing and unhappy.

Why are they so unhappy? Cheer up!
The cops eye her up like that too, but the men
she dates would never be caught dead looking like
they desire anything: sort of bored. They all look
sort of bored. Maybe this is all about boredom or
growth hormones in the chickens. She's been really
sad lately. At 32, you're truly thirty. She wants that fucking
mango mouse. Damn it. Is everyone a thief?
At that point the cameras stop rolling, and the critics
say this poem is like *Weeds* or *Orange is the New Black*.
It is a poem white people can really identify with. Don't
they all sleep with black street dealers, then quote a poem
they read when they were at Sarah Lawrence? It's all so
post-race. When will the people outside Brooklyn
get it? It's all *post,* except the black kids ought
to wear loafers if they don't want to get shot.
You can do anything you want to, as long as you
know how to dress, and the white people she knows
are all cool, and not racists, or sexists, or anything like that,
except if you live with them, and you have something tasty
in the fridge, they co-opt it and they don't even say they're
sorry, and if you say, "Hey Katie, did you take my mango mousse?"
they all say: "Get a life, bitch," and go out the door with their
little shit of a boyfriend who's always buying records
by Bulgarian punk bands, and calling his black friends
"my *nigs.*" Perhaps that's it. Everyone is so casual
they are all *grocking,* and being *grocked,* but
she's sad, with her big ass, and her hair turning
frizzy in the rain, and she wonders if there is not some
black in her genes, and maybe she's like mixed race?
Her friend tells her white women are oppressed
so they don't have to wish they were black. It's all so
confusing. She wants sushi. She wants something
with a little heat in it. She catches a glimpse of her
ass in the window of a store. Sadness is everywhere.

I take my gun and shoot her. It's a mercy killing.
When they ask me why, I say
I felt frightened of her privilege. I am wearing loafers.
Everyone is shocked. They say: but he always recycled.
It's true, then they shoot me, and in spite of all my
readings, my knowledge of George Trakl's poetry, my
stirring lecture on certain textural abnormalities in the
late poems of George Herbert, I turn back into what
I have always been (like the wolf man):
a white cop, a white cop who thinks
he has done no one any harm. But that's a lie. I am
not a cop. What do I know about deadly force? Isn't that
what I pay taxes for? I feel bad I shot my digression.
She wasn't real. Sooner or later, they're all constructs:
the brutal police, the black young kid in sneakers, the
thirty something white girls still living with roommates,
those who understand, those who don't, the disaffected
elephants, the snide rhinos, the Bulgarian punk bands,
the erudite store clerks, quoting Adorno. All of it is so
tentative—between minor and major modes.
Oh, strike the piercing chord!
Be a body wholly body, dressed in rags.
Play the pianissimo of three—sound
of the rain on a highway, mercy is everywhere, but you
have to sit still and let it sniff your hand. You have to let it
know you've stopped biting. Your teeth have fallen out
like the snow of fangs the prophets spoke of:
And the sharp teeth of the world will fall softly
silently as snow, and there will be singing and chanting
in the streets—lion and lamb, and no one will be
anyone anymore except quiet, vast as the sky. Then
the dead will bury the dead. Then Rachel will cease
weeping for her children. She will say:
Dance on the body of my sadness
until you break its bones.

Poem in Which I Am Both Grateful and Ungrateful

It's stupid to miss working in a factory.
I mean the pay sucked, and the hours?
11:30 to 8 am (didn't get paid for lunch).
And the foremen walked about like
cops on a beat, and were by turns
friendly and sadistic and
ended up having messy affairs
with the women in finished inspection
who were always *girls*—even though
they were never girls
and the foremen were married
and half the girls were married
and sometimes they were married
to men on another shift—
and all of that was shit because
wherever love is lacking
a will to power comes to fill the void
and power in that stinking joint
meant you got to be mean without
someone being mean back at you.
It's where I learned to hate *power*,
not authority. Hipsters can hate authority.
I hate power, which unlike authority,
isn't satisfied with running things.
It has to reward and punish, and mostly
for no real fucking reason at all—
like some hand that strokes and slaps,
but, I digress. I was never allowed to digress
in the factory and so I'm digressing now:
I hated power but I loved the pierogis
that the Polish guys gave me in finished grinding
and the spring rolls the Vietnamese guys
gave me in CNC milling,
and the Neck Bones and chopped barb

I got from the black guys who'd
come up in the sixties from North Carolina
and ran rough grinding,
and I loved the ox tail soup, the little shots
of Espiritus and homemade flavored vodka
and I loved the loading dock
whose door was so thick it could
shut out all but the hum of the machines,
and there you'd be, on the dock
by the dumpsters, sucking down three cigs
for a fifteen minute break, watching the red glowing
eyes of the fat raccoons, their graceful paws dumpster
diving, and the moon above you
making the forsythia out there god knows why
glow with a supernatural light,
and maybe just a few stars—passed the
halogen lights, and I'd stand there and smoke
and God would speak to me like Abram
calling me to his covenant, making his promises
of vast and small, small and vast who are
forever married, who
lie in the heart, producing whole tribes of longing
and I'd step on my cig, bow to the moon
then go back in
to that noise, which was *clamor*—a hundred
noise bands jerking off.

And the poles didn't always like the blacks,
and the blacks didn't like the Vietnamese
who they thought acted stuck up
and the Vietnamese guys never let the foremen
divide them, and worked together,
and when one fell behind on his rate,
another would give him labor tickets.
And the Spanish guys from Colombia

taught me ghost stories about a woman
ghost who lurked at bridges and beat
men who cheated on their wives
half to death, and one guy would lift
up his shirt, and show me a nasty scar and
say: "her teeth were sharp, but she didn't
like the cognac in my blood," and he'd laugh
displaying three gold teeth, and shit, I
was often amused, and they called me El Blanco
because I was the only American born
white guy in the plant, and they called me
B and M (for Bitching and Moaning) because
I was the steward, and wrote their grievances,
and ended up teaching them to write and read
English, and showed up for hearings on Green cards,
and went to funerals and baptisms where my pale
Irish working class ass stood out, as Leon put
it, like "lint on a brown suit." And everyone
was always feeding me, feeding me, and cursing me,
and we'd talk. And someone would say:
"Weil, why you here? You're a dumb shit in
everything but books." and I'd say:
"I like the food."
To be the only American born white guy
in a three block plant is to learn
if only in the small, not the vast, what it
means to be cut free of your tribe,
to no longer be "in power," to see the
white managers walking past you as if
you were a ghost and hear them speak
of golf, and a bike rally and vacations in
Mexico, and you're dirty and not them, thank God,
not them, but you're not your co-workers, either.
You're what? God's grace, the voice heard
in Sumeria, under the stars that says:

66

"Be cut off at the stem, free fall into my arms."
And I believe in God, and I believe I am a fuck-up,
one with all the race of fuck-ups, and that
God understands, and that God is not a foremen
hired by the moralists to beat me, and I believe
in laughing when Tai said to me:
"Americans…they get mad if the moon doesn't
come down from the sky and give them a blow job."
And I thought about that, and just laughed
and said: *The truth makes me laugh.*
And I learned in those 20 years not to get mad
at the moon if it didn't come down, but some nights
I swear I ascended, and floated above National Tool,
until all the machines became silent, and the
silence held me, and God is not a foremen, and
God is not a boss. Authority is not power.
It can live in the red eyes of raccoons, in the
waxy yellow of forsythia, in the heaviness
of your shoes. That's what I miss because
I am grateful not to stink, I guess, and not to
be called shit head, cracker, jerk wad, scumbag—
get back to your machine. But in the world where
I labor now, everything is white. The black folks
and the Asians are white.
Everything is white the way I learned not to be
white—white in power, in the soft spoken
sociopathy of careers, white with white
and I am afraid I will be hurled from this
heaven of white down to the closed factories,
the ruined gardens of the poor,
and only because I am bad at
expecting the moon to come down
and give me a blow job, and I am bad at
"success" which I see as a creature of
power and not of authority—an unnatural

lying beast, wearing the face of some cute
Disney character, whispering this and inferring
this—not from God, but willing to use a God.
A thing I fear and hate and know I must become,
a thing I fear and hate and know I must become
unless I can find enough time to swallow my own
spit and look at my babies, and say: not even for you,
but if not for them, then who? Slowly Abram mounted
his ass—neither too slowly, for this would have been
resentment, nor too quickly, for this would
have been a sick zeal, a fanatic's lust,
and rode off toward the mountain with Isaac.
And Isaac said: Father, where is the sacrifice?
And Abram said: God will provide it.
What angel might stay my hand? How to
saddle the ass and ride? Fuck if I know.
Tears dry up. Sleep is a forgotten pleasure.
The graves of the poor are full of bouncing checks
with losing lottery tickets, and all my relatives.
I am a good teacher, a lousy academic,
bad at promoting my art, bad at schmoozing,
and the food isn't good here: it's all indifferent
hummus, and nothing is fried or tasty, and
I must not be hearing the truth because I
can't remember the last time I laughed
that loud, or shouted above the clamor.
What I miss is my failure—the sustainable
failure. Wall Street would throw me to the wolves.
The vast smallness of my being is crying for
something small—not all this shit.
Wouldn't I laugh if, say, a full professor
came toward me with a slight gut, bearing
a plastic shot glass of Espirtus, and a
pierogi wrapped in cheese cloth and said:
"B&M! The wife says thanks for helping me

68

with that paper." Fuck it. It ain't gonna happen.
I am an alien here, and an alien in the factory, too.
This knife feels strange in my hand. The angel
is taking his sweet fucking time. Akabah!
Bind me fast, Lord, lest I resist.

I Am Whatever Early Pasternak Said

That's right. I am the black spring,
the slush of melting snow.
I am two elks locking horns.
And the whistle of an eternal long ago.
I am...well? A mushroom stove.
and I, of course, I want the world to work out right
beyond graduate students and plumbers
and the swifts who dive through chimneys
and who nest
beyond the obvious tropes: the red selvage in the west.
Somewhere, the signature of a skate disappears,
whatever was inscribed, the figure 8 of the years.
She moves as an alder moves. She moves through tears.

Linked Masturbation Haiku

Scrill of sun rise.
Friend's mom stands touching herself
in the hallway: I look hard.

Nails against her robe,
red, and the blue silk moving
to and fro and

No one wants a poem
like this. This is America:
geese, angry nuns.

Yes guns, not sex!
But she's wonderful!
Pull love's trigger, ma. Bang!

The sky is falling.
Her robe is falling.
Oak floor, blue silk: smooch.

Up comes her girlfriend
from behind, cupping
one breast, agile, friendly. Hi.

Me—16, forlorn.
I cough, feign sleep
like deer, turn head and bolt.

Son still asleep.
I never tell him through
pancakes eggs and toast.

Your ma was touching herself—
all folks touch themselves,
and if not—good for them.

No doubt he knows.
He has a pet ferret.
What wouldn't he know?

I touch myself.
Faint stink of ferret,
the moon still visible.

Why write this poem?
It is friendly, well disposed.
That's why.

40 years later.
He's dead. She's 72.
Bathroom still full of swans.

Fire Birds

I don't believe in peace.
Peace is for folks with
money and bird feeders.
I don't believe in serenity.
It's a racket, like leisure wear.
I dreamed last night there were
skulls under the yoga mat,
severed hands.
How do I go on like this?
I go on like this.
For peace there are
piece rates.
Everyone is supposed to
produce a given amount
of peace per square foot.
I am behind on my quota.
Soon they will come for
me with peace cleavers
and serenity axes
their yoga pants outlawed
in Montana.
They will say: "You're not
being positive."
They will cut my throat
for peace, drink my blood
for bird twitter, the very
nice people in Chatham
and Oakpark will come
against me. I can feel it
in their lawns. In every
Ranch style and Cape Cod
house a hundred peace guns
are waiting to go off. I
am in the cross hairs.

What Must I Do, Mary Oliver?
I sat on a lawn all night with a
sugar cube, but not one
grasshopper came to sup
from my proffering hand.
It must be my attitude.
Instead, lepers, and former
baton twirlers from a thousand
trailer parks showed. I fed
them all, but I had no peace.
Just this sword—this fire
in my blood, from which
two figures were dancing.
Can you see them?
They fox trot from the furnace.
They don't shut it down,
and they don't lie to their
windows, saying: "Hey, look!
An Eastern Gold Finch!"
Well, maybe they do.
(Even I have been known to say:
Look! An eastern gold finch!
It's only human) but
the neat lawn is a savannah.
The Eastern Gold finch
is purchased with blood.
None of this is peace.
All of it is calamity,
a conflagration, I see
all of it burning.
The cats see it, too.
They sit at the French windows,
ears up, tails a-twitch, waiting
for the fire birds to land.

Memorial Day

There is nothing to be done.
You scout the grass for signs
of that American busy on which
usually, you hang your brains:
but *no*.

The to do list ran off
with your first wife, then your second.
Your current live-in girlfriend has you
crushing soft cans of beer and pitching
them over the neighbor's bushes at the stray cat.
Her toes nails are painted purple with
little daisies on them. She says she's
"Spontaneous." She says she wants to
move to Arizona.
She claims an astrologer told her
she would find her path in Arizona.

You're almost 48 and dubious of paths.
Even those which are constantly swept
and lead to brick patios are
blighted. The cat stares at you. You stare
at the cat. You do not like cats, but this one?
He's more than a cat. He's the nemesis you need.
Dandelions are no longer a challenge.
The neighbors became tolerable after their
19 year old son was killed.
They stopped having parties. They stopped
gardening while playing the Smiths.
They moved out, and for the time being,
you have no neighbors to your right and
the ones to your left are more righteous than you,
less tolerant of other people's noises,
likely to call the cops and to say they didn't.

You stare at the cat and pitch another can.
He must know what you need because
he comes over and purrs, rubs against
your naked leg, swishes his tail,
sinks his fangs and claws into your
shoulder. "Fuck!" you cry,
and you are chasing him, leaping
over bushes, racing through
backyards—jumping the pools,
becoming a young man, then a baby,
then nothing at all. The cat rests and
licks his still unneutered balls.

The pregnant woman, your mother,
is putting a little too much whiskey in her
sun tea. It's 1966. The war is on TV.
She loves Stan Getz. She loves Leonard Nimoy.
She wants to grab him by his Vulcan ears
while he fucks her.

Your girlfriend wonders where you've gone, but is
not too displeased. After all, you've let
yourself go. Your paunch
casts a shadow over her sandals. You're
a mess, and she has plans. Your mother, too.
Everyone has plans. Past, present, future.
Only the cat knows how to lie
in the grass, in a certain slant of light,
eyeing the grazing cow birds
until, when he feels like it, he'll strike,
bringing the bird sans head to your
door—bloody, disjointed, placing it
there, in your absence, a sort of memorial.

This Ain't UNICEF

And out of the world wound,
six blow flies,
and perhaps a string quartet

and 4 comfortable academics frowning,
speaking of "oppression"
in theoretical words that

are difficult to carry on the 32 bus
which the far from theoretical woman has just missed.
Dumb fucking bitch is what her boss says.

We all know that phrase: "Dumb fucking bitch." It is recalled
at the working class studies conference. Everyone wants an
end to humiliation or perhaps at the very least

a symposium on it (for why not have endless symposiums?)
Excuse me, but I own the chief research on this
phrase which scans as / / U / : Dumb Fucking Bitch

It cannot be said in the higher precincts of our economy.
Only amid the retrograde, the failed, those for whom a
missed bus is a missed day is a missed rent is a—

but I digress, I am
not able to stay on task, something inside me wobbles
and out of the wound comes the seven

deadly sins or dwarfs or virtues (take your pick) but what bothers
me is how the boss says it—without even the benefit of anger
or any doubt as to the veracity of his utterance as if it

has been written on her forehead: in day glow letters: and she only stands there, arms folded, and is told to take her shit and get the fuck out of there, back on the bus which is now too

late instead of too early, and on which she is short a quarter and has to ask around until someone gives her the change. And the bus driver says: *hurry up, lady, this ain't UNICEF.*

Non-poem

It has wooden slats (Norwegian wood, I submit)
with two black stirrups where the feet most likely go,
like skis—only not, and a pulley with what look like
bike handles or the handles on boxer's jump ropes.

I want to paint little shamanistic signs on the wood slats,
then get long wire, cello strings, perhaps, and
string them from the black leather hobby horse
to the bass of the machine: securing it all with a nail gun.

I want to turn it into a harp, except the pulley will pull
tinkling shards of bottle glass along, that barely touch,
thus making the sound of ice being shaken in a perfect rocks glass
by a person you want and can never have—

This is what I think about almost all the time. You believe I am
thinking about politics, or Fidel Castro's scratchy beard moving
along the thighs of Barbara Walters, or maybe I am thinking
about how Merle Oberon's breath smelled bad for all her beauty,
or about being in that rock and mineral room as a child when all
the lights were out. The rocks glowed and they said: "You are not alone"
and I believed them but I am not thinking about that at all, that dross,
that detritus, which, well you know, stuff.

I am thinking how at the end of the semester when my grades
are all in and there is nothing to do but wait for the solstice, I will
create this gigantic sound out of what was once a Nordic Track. It will
set it up in the yard as a sound sculpture though none of my neighbors
will approve, nor the art critics like it, or even the deer and skunks
who come to eat my veggies. Does it matter? Must it be liked?

Much folly has been proven wise. Sooner or later, unlike Plato,
unlike Keats, I will attempt my pure realm thoughts. Help me.
Help me build my Lyre! Come with sea shells and tinkling ornaments.
Come, moving beyond the middle range of poets who never...

Fuck it. I will not finish my sentence. I am down here on the porch waiting for the first lightning bugs. Maybe a calico dress empty of all but the dusk will join me, and a banjo. Who knows? I have bought a nail gun, wire, the strangeness of my tribe.
Anything could happen, and it probably won't.

In Memory of *Tony Gotta Dance*

I want to win the lottery, but I don't play it
which cuts down on the odds.
Sometimes I miss the old guys from my neighborhood
still using Vitalis in their hair, refusing ever to wear jeans.
(My dad said jeans were for boys, not men).
I remember they were always buying scratch-offs.
It got so that the wait in the bodega
resembled an unemployment line.

Now-a-days they mail the check to you.
No one wants to see a line four blocks long unless
it's for the premier of *The Hunger Games*.

This isn't a poem. This is a "TED talk." I like to talk. It
doesn't take a Fulbright. All the old guys
are mostly dead or dying, but the scratch-offs remain.
Hope lingers with addiction. Hope and addiction could
have been the name of a pop group on my street. I
have had my share of both.

I don't play the lottery because I always expect to win.
It's never casual with me. That ticket sings in my wallet:
"You can quit! You can fish for char in Iceland. You can run
your own bodega and rip up all the tabs. You can give the kids
free ice cream. You can sit playing cards in the sun!"

But the best I ever did was two numbers out of six. Louise,
with your dream book full of winners, I salute you.
And *Tony Gotta Dance*, I miss the smell of your Vitalis
how you never left the factory in anything less than a suit.
You were our bookie. You came in each morning blowing
rings of cigar smoke, whistling Sinatra. You once told me you
knew Frankie Valli back in the day, and that he was "a solid."
I believe you. I believe he was a solid. And you? You always
made the vig.

The world is a shit hole, Tony. Your son was sick and
died at 32. Your wife was dead. Your cigars were cheap.
Towards the end, you stopped changing into a suit but
you still wore those polished Italian shoes. They buried you
in them. I went. Tony, I'm a solid, not a stripe,
drove 200 miles down from Binghamton to see you laid to rest.
I saw the pictures of your wife. She looked
like every pretty girl from the neighborhood circa 1954.
You were a looker, too. Tony, they don't have lines anymore.
They've hidden the war, and they've hidden the lines.

Remember that lay off in '86? I was a young kid then.
You came to the line with your betting slips and a bottle of Jack.
You gave everyone a taste. You took their bets,
and you and me sang harmony on "I Only Have Eyes for You."
You remember? You don't remember—
shit. "All stiffs plead the fifth." That's how you used to put it.
Tony Gotta Dance, you're a stiff. I'm talking to a dead man.
But I was always crazy, you know.
You were so alive in '86, your silver hair slicked back—
your good baritone on display. You made what sucked
seem almost like a party. Though we all knew better.
God rest your Sinatra whistling ass. The world has lost
its color. They all wear dress casual
(the jeans cost more than your suits).
But it's alright, if there's a heaven for small time bookies,
I hope you're there—tipping huge, your wad in a diamond
studded money clip, Sinatra on the juke box,
and every cigar a genuine Havana.

May Day

I keep an old drill bit I once sharpened at a 135, to push through twelve inches of number 4 stainless steel. 118 is the standard, figured out by Ford's tool makers around 1910. At 135, a drill bit pushes more than cuts. You take an oil stone to its cutting edge, slightly dull it so that push and cut will work together, and then the drill won't "walk," won't break off in the hole (well, most of the time). I took the bit home with me one night as a souvenir. I was so tired I fell asleep standing up at my machine and dropped it on my Knapps: this was a two inch diameter bit. It's heavy. Its long. It hurts. Steel toes saved my sleepy ass. I saw feet crushed from the dropping of half ton plates, saw a young boy's fingers severed clean by a steel plate's edge. All around us, mangled toes, slipped disks, hands dyed by years of cutting oil. Arthritis in long ago injured joints, tendons tightened so badly from heavy lifts, that we called the old timers "puppet arms." The arms of these men would be slightly hoisted up. They couldn't rest them at their sides. "Look at that bald mother fucker! Hey! Asks him where the strings be hangin! Hey puppet man! Puppet man! Come over here and give daddy a nice big blow job." Everything was a nice big blow job. "Boy, don't you know the bosses dick be up your stank? You hear me? You think you special? You talk that poetry, but daddy hear a mumble. Talk pretty with them balls in your mouth. Go ahead baby. Take them cum shots. They like it when you swallow."

The drill survived four moves, two layoffs, a "teaching career." Sometimes I feel a throb where my right index finger was lopped down to the bone. The drill bit is my Excalibur. When I die, some old puppet arm's going to come and fetch it. He'll wander the earth looking for a chuck to lock it down. A jig bore will rise, dripping, from the lake. Till then I can hear the screams of that young man. Calmly I bagged four of his fingers. Two they reattached. Two others were only severed at the top. *No big deal* he said, when he came back to work and we took him out to drink. "It's just the tops." It was only after ten shots of peppermint schnapps that he was throwing up against the car and then he cried. "Look what they did to me." I'm not there anymore. A friend says: "Look at you!" Yes. *Look at me.* In the middle of someone name dropping Chomsky, in the middle of another Agamben spiel, I hear the diamond cutter dressing the grinding wheel. I forget. I forget where I am. I forget my student. He has just written a really bad Sestina. "Weil," I hear. "Break's over…*get back to your machine.*"

Whenever He Enters These Cut Ones

At sixteen, I entered the sublime
and read nothing but Rilke for six months straight.
I felt elevated, floated passed the Amoco
like some preening swan, picking the algae
of lesser thoughts from my pure white breast.

My dad said certain snobs were not to be dismissed
if they could play Bach with the fingers of a god,
or rhyme the universe with cheese,
but their followers? Oh, they were miserable fucks,
and made life harder than it needed to be.

What are you doing? I'm existing in the ineffable.
Sounds like a plan: Good luck. Take out the trash.
Rilke had castles. I had the White Castle
which, late at night, deserted in the snow except
for one old drunk clutching his coffee like a talisman
was truly ineffable: an ongoing Night Hawks.

Use what you got: dirt, sky, dog, tree,
the vital ugliness through which gods pour
down from their height, beyond a sense of taste.
The world grows pure by such impiety.

Beauty tears the law. Remember that.
Don't mistake curtains for covenant.
The Roman soldiers, sacking the temple found
only the Torah, a miserable scroll.
And the U.S. Cavalry, having routed some starving Sioux,
found only grass, and bone in the sacred bag.

What are we to do with grass and bone?
Or the five books of the Torah, or that old drunk
so down and out, his own coffee doesn't like him?
No longer let wooing shape your cry.

God whispers from the sidewalks.
Or God is just some lie the literary elite made
before they turned to reading Marcel Proust.

Remember the Bishop who stooped to wash
the beggar's feet. And the beggar kicked him
knocked his miter askew, and said,
Now you're like me, and I'm like you:
kicked and bleeding, and in pain.
No need to thank me, Bishop. *Humility comes free.*

Night Shift

for the Angel Raphael

When I had one egg in the fridge
with a dirty finger print on it,
compliments of the night shift,
I said wearily to the kitchen:
I'll never get away with murder.
It was an inside joke. I was
inside my apartment. It was inside
the enclosed space of 7 am—
winter, the light just starting to
rise—all the windows smudged
with light—
sort of, sort of a sun rise, my hair
already thinning, hands covered
in grinding dust.

I considered boiling the egg.
Instead I put on Mahler's 9th,
made myself a night shift drink:
Amaretto with milk. I was
disgusting. The job was disgusting,
and the bell ringing from the church up the
street was pure. A pure tolling. Someone
had died and there was a mass with
a polished hearse ready to escort
the dead. I fell asleep
at the kitchen table and dreamed
the corpse took the egg,
boiled it in my speckled sauce pan,
touched my forehead with it:
a coolness, an anointing
of the sick.

It was an act of love. Wake up,
the light decreed. I roused
and glimpsed the angel fleeing.
When I opened the fridge the egg
was still there—complete with the
dirty finger print. I lived another day
and then the next, watched
old men in the bodega playing
dominoes, watched the pin oak
hold its leaves. The prayer said
"that we may not be as strangers
in the province of joy…" And I believed
that day and the next—something—
though its name was treacherous,
and its spell of mercy always
waiting to be broken.

Horse Chestnut

Out of your seed a milky foam mingled
with rain water and turned the linens a soft sky blue,
and under your heavy boughs, casks of Bavarian
beer cooled by the ice of glacial
lakes once stood there shaded and at rest.

As a child I stripped your nuts of their spiked
green breast plates and threw them at
the other kids, collecting them in
a red wagon, loving the glossy brown
and the sparrow buff of their hard bodies.

Anne Frank dreamed you from her hiding place
in the center of Amsterdam, longed to spin
under your blooms, the flowers, white then marked
a pink grown into red—and, yet in clusters,
the flowers remain a trumpeting of spring.

And, when the tree she wrote of died around
the time she would have been an old woman,
they raised you from the dead, though Anne remained
young, annihilated by stupidity,
by men who have no time for mercy or for trees   /.

Who has no time for mercy or for trees?
Why are we alive? I ask the obvious
barely willing to entertain more novel
interrogations. An old wino, his socks off,
sitting under your branches drinking Night

Train is a god, and the child lifting nuts
to toss them at a friend is a god,
and the brittle ocher of your oversized leaves
in Autumn are unspectacular
in their final color as your flowers are

spectacular in their first. Those, too, are
gods, gods everywhere—crumbled into leaf dust,
the tiny fists of children crushing them.
And so I break these gods against all that
has no time for mercy or for trees.

You, the tree of Kiev, witness to kissing
and to pogroms, tree whose leaves I first saw
dappling the ceilings of my grandmother's
house and reached out for from my crib:
Panicles of your flowers as erect

as the young boy underneath you touching
the stem of his longing, at the scar where
the leaf is torn: a horse shoe with its seven
nails, its seven marks of wintering blows,
one each for the virgin's seven sorrows.

A Story

I was told by my crazy uncle Pete
that there were men so lost to this world
they became the evening's air.
Shut up kid and listen.
We'd sit on his porch, he with his Rheingold,
me with my juice glass (mostly fully of suds).
Listen hard. He promised
they'll start singing.
Singing what?
"The gibberish of God."

He told me the stars spoke Yiddish.
"The stars are the ghosts of Jewish cobblers.
They sit on their stools
and cobble the shoes of heaven."

"A good cobbler never talks.
He's listening to his hammer.
He's hearing the cry of God in the leather.
He's doing his job."

And what about the men who become the air?

Uncle Pete took a sip of his beer.
"They're doing their job, too.
Why do you think you can breathe?
All the real work of love is invisible and thankless."

I listened but couldn't hear.
"Someday," he said. "The song will be silence."
The crickets grew louder around us.
Ball games could be heard
from screen porches up the block.
Koufax was always striking out the side.
Brock was stealing third.
The Mets were mostly losing.

One day a man gets so lost, he told me
that his arms become a breeze
that moves through the white flowers
of spring orchards. His eyes become rain,
beating against the macadam.
His voice is the yellow light that lives
in the windows of passing trains.
Then he is ready to be the air.

"It's an apprenticeship," he told me.

I listened, knowing he was lying.

I kiss my son's forehead.
Kissing it again, and again kissing
it, I say: "Shemah, Israel."
I am hearing the air all around us,
and the ceaseless cobbling of stars.

Blessed Are the Merciful

The kid they hired as assistant
to the shop floor engineer
didn't understand he was there
not to be good with numbers
but to fire men. They called it
efficiency, streamlining, cutting
the fat. He liked to talk to me.
I knew he was a wayward missile then
and would only harm himself.

He loved his knowledge the way
autistic children do. Obsessed
with World War II, he explained
in detail how the Germans lost the war
because a ball bearing in their tanks
was not designed to withstand
the Russian winter. "It cracked,"
he said, "it was a crack in a ball bearing,
not the crack of a rifle
that halted the juggernaut."

I thought how mercy sleeps
even in our efficiency, and wakes
only to seep through the flaws,
a slow ooze of incompetence.
A child poor at irony, he was
pure in his mission, and when
he discovered the plant manager
was selling scrapped plates to
some wise guys out the door
he presented his information cleanly
and was duly fired, not knowing
the human machine works
by a series of design flaws.

He cried in my arms, which wasn't easy,
considering he was six feet tall.
I held him awkwardly, knowing this dumb
fuck was good in the way that mountains
are, incapable of pretending to be
a river. "You're not an asshole,"
I said, my highest compliment.
I was crying, too. The guys called me
faggot for a month. "Hey Weil,
want to hug me?" He was management
and didn't see the invisible fault line
that cut the ground between us.
I erased it with my sorrow
grown into his baffled shame.
I grafted to his tree, his tap root
flailing in mid-air.
For a year I thought of him,
the way he would smile goofy at
a drill bit or a reamer, knowing
the machinist's hand book by heart,
knowing the secret of what destroys
a German offensive, this little defective
part inside the swiftest Panzer.
I gave him my Brown and Sharpe
Micrometer—the one from 1890.

A week later, they hired a guy who
knew he wasn't there to see the numbers,
to see the truth—to *see*.
20 men were gone inside a month
to pay for the "inventory."
Another 20 by the next. I survived
by hiding on the night shift and
doing my peon's dance.
The plant manager flourished.
The wise guys got their scrap.

94

I often think of what sleeps
inside me, this flaw through
which mercy seeps—a moment's
reprieve from the shape shifting
of survival. Confound the juggernaut.
Lay low the machinery of men
who only look the other way. Sweet Christ,
hold up thy serpents eye that I might meet it,
and be healed of my affliction.
Have mercy on me, have mercy on me.
Have mercy on me, have mercy on me—
I who have so little mercy.
Who have only the weight of my enemy's
tears to carry on my shoulder.

Vibrant Monday Poem in Which Certain Things Almost Occur

The wind in Emily's hair
is not the wind in my hair,
(which is an absence of hair)
nor is it the wind in the hair
of, let us say, Rapunzel,
nor the wind-tossed hair
of vibrant young smokers
in commercials 50 years ago,
their hair tousled
to the fresh, breezy country
taste of…Kool?

This wind in Emily's hair
is going to blow south
like some minor Greek god
who makes the daffodils rise.
Why not? It is Monday
and if I want to write about
the wind in my wife's hair
then, damn it, I shall.

I am giddy with writing it:
It is fun to say "Shall."
It makes me feel pretentious
(in a good way) as if
I am wearing expensive
Italian shoes, and playing
a Beckstein grand.
It is grand to say shall.
The wind is blowing
through all the shalls
of this world, and it,
the vital it of the wind
has made my eyes
dizzy with pleasure.

Touch her hair, says the
stage prompter, but
I've grown shy, and walk
too fast, as if trying not
to get mugged by my own
desire, which is vast
like the hatch of may flies,
like a great flock
of red winged blackbirds,
like...well, I'm stalling!
Touch her hair, shit-head,
But I don't. I walk on until
she says: hey, and I halt.
Someday I will be dead.
This is not an unhappy
thought, but a fact and
the wind will blow
through the long luxuriant
hair of my grave (thank
Whitman). Right now I
am very much alive,
walking too fast for
my wife who takes her time
and rightfully so.
It is Sunday, and we are
playing hooky from children
to see a flick called "Enemies."
I will remember this hour
until I grow senile which
may be any day now. I
will remember the wind
in her dark hair and the
way I no longer cared about
being original or intelligent.
As I halt, she catches up

and takes my hand, not even
mildly annoyed, knowing I
am a nervous body set
loose upon the earth—an
urban sprawl. We take our time
together. To quote the captain:
Let it be so.

Leo Tolstoy: The Death of Ivan Ilyich

The Blessing

...and they were buying and selling, and giving and taking in marriage unto the last hour, and were caught unaware...

The Gospel

Don't you know that a midnight hour comes when everyone has to take off his mask? Do you think life always lets itself be trifled with? Do you think you can sneak off a little before midnight to escape this?

Soren Kierkegaard

It is as if I had been going downhill while I imagined I was going up. And that is really what it was. I was going up in public opinion, but to the same extent life was ebbing away from me. And now it is all done and there is only death.

What had ceased was comfort.
It took on the shape and stink
of sloth.

It looked like men loafing
laying down
at rest.

A simulacrum of comfort—

a virus that had infected the
body of suffering

and made it appear

"at ease," ordinary in its pleasures.

And so we constructed the happy poor

lazy and singing and fucking and

we know the rest.

Work was the cure—work that
kept them busy.

The true sloth
which loves nothing
hates nothing
feels nothing
wants nothing
stays busy
because it is nothing

rose from that nest
and lived in the eyes
of sales clerks.

Maranatha! The inward groaning cried

ten thousand feet below this crust of "doing."

After considering slashing its throat

sloth left the cry alone, thought
it would die out,

take on a shape of being:

buy, sell, ring out the customers

ring in the New Year, no longer

hear itself.

And so Christ descended into hell.

If there is hope,

it is that, having heard what has been left to die,

the master rose

buried under all false prayers.

He Hears—who walk about pretending

to be alive: let us know that we are sick.

Let us know that we are sick.

This is the first blessing

and the last.

The Greeting

Who is this living in the funeral and the stone
and in this vague spirit among the trees—
so like a patch of snow come early spring
remnant and outs-lander
afterthought that rises:

quick to break—a wave or its curled shadow?
Between them, wherever being stands
poised at its vanishing, so too, the ground
begins to waver, opens

cracked, broken—not law, but spirit moving.
A man grasps a shovel, his hands smoothed
with dirt and begins to bury himself,
yet he will not stay put
will not cease from moving—

the quick plunge of birds through the morning's
drifting fog—the sound of hello so strange
to his ears, as if he had just now entered speech
and must answer with his life.

I Was a Good Son

The shit I cleaned between my mother's legs
and the sight of her—golden, drinking a whiskey sour
are not commensurate. Nothing will be commensurate again.
And if I should build one of those cozy deaths, who am I as
a poet? We all die badly. The stain of love is upon the new born
leaf: the first pimple in my infant's cheek. Am I to
dismiss the flawed world for this whore we call perfection?
My mother kept saying, *you're a good son* through the morphine,
and I kept saying: *don't die.*
Both of us stupid and fierce—Oh God, she was so fierce.
The fingers of the dying can break bones.

How do I tell her I wanted to fuck girls. I wanted to
escape into flannel shirts and beer, become whatever
it was that was not her dying. Even now I am
ashamed, and say: I was a good son. I was a good son.
What I was is love and love is not good. It is not dutiful.
It does not "Stay the course." It breaks like a cheap watch.
I was a cheap watch, Ma, forgive me. I was a cheap watch
and both of us were lying.

Something

Those are trees you see
over there
and most days you don't notice
them
except if they were gone
you'd have to squint more.
Towards the east
as you backed out of your drive.
You know now that's a white birch.
The ice has bent it to its will
but the rest is, well, just trees:
some kind of pine, and from
what you know, some kind of
maple, given the leaves
that clog your roof gutters.
One day you look and
the birch is gone.
Why this guilt, this weird
sharp grief you feel
as if your own indifference
had cut it down? Sometimes
when you're tired
and the day goes badly
you think that birch
might have made a difference
like the stone you used to hold
pressed against your forehead,
that cooling rock
when your parents fought—
just that. It's not
enough, but it was something.

CPSIA information can be obtained
at www.ICGtesting.com
Printed in the USA
LVHW041331190723
752896LV00019B/217